Alison Haw

Castle Clothes

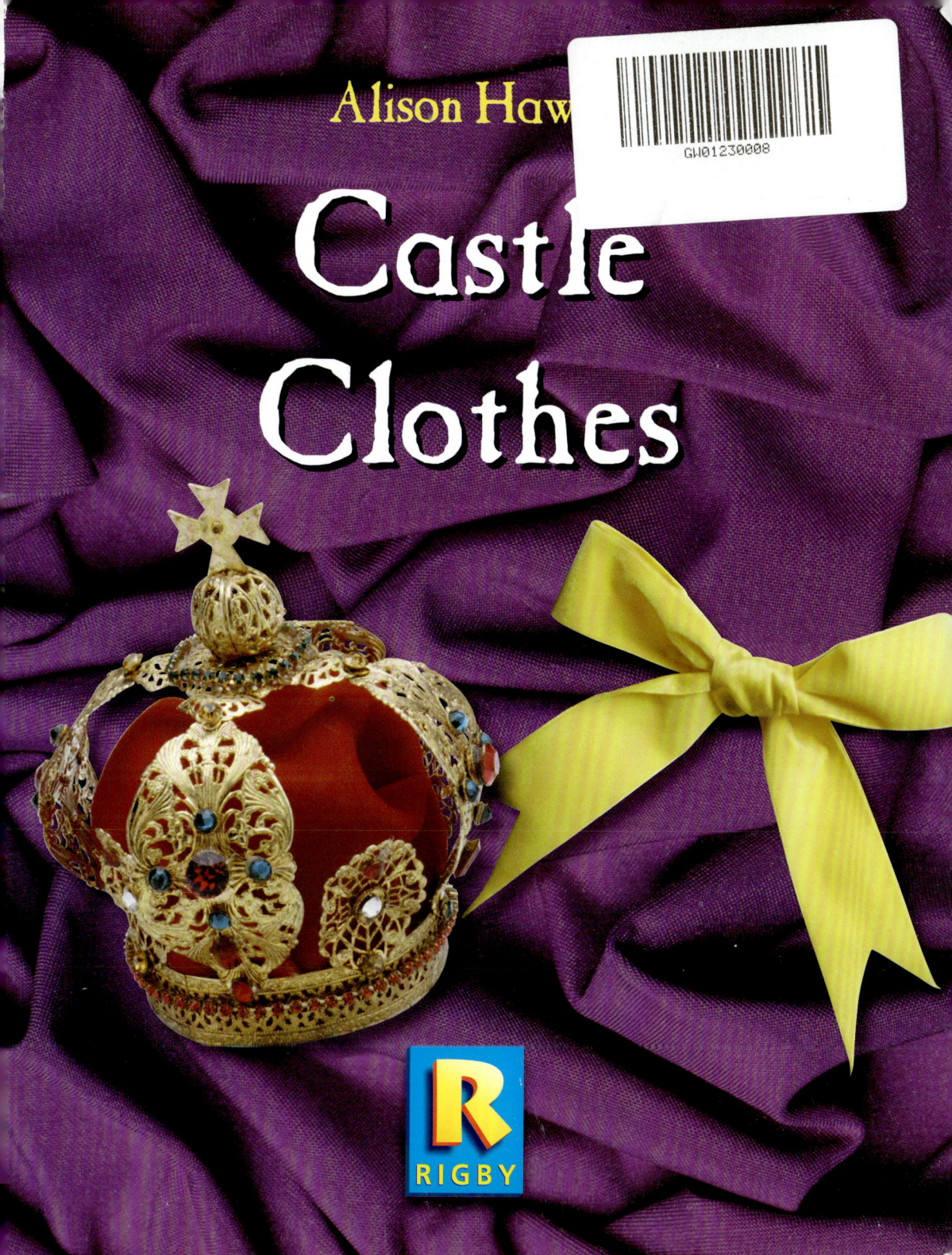

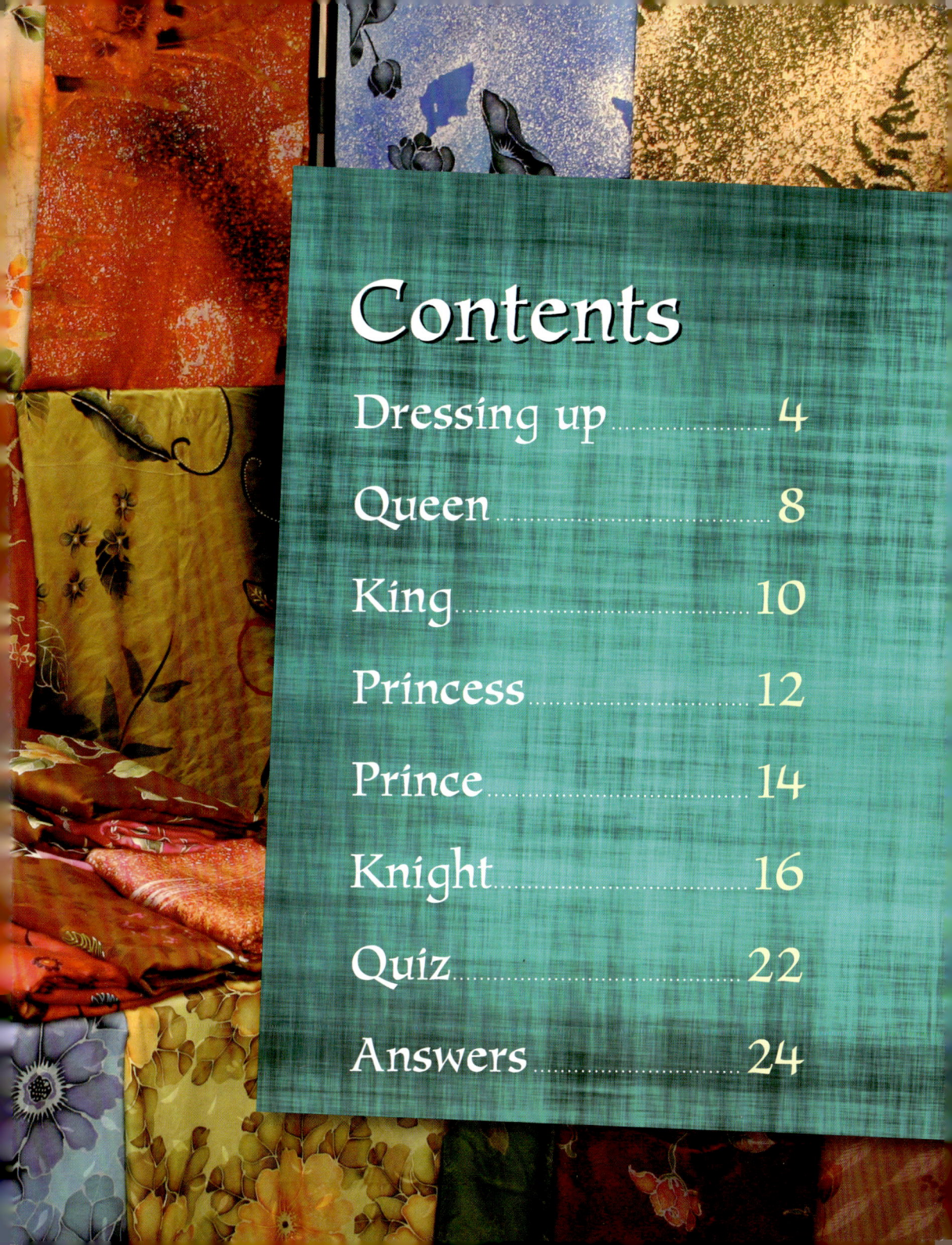

Contents

Dressing up 4

Queen 8

King 10

Princess 12

Prince 14

Knight 16

Quiz 22

Answers 24

Dressing up

It is fun to dress up in different clothes.

You can dress up as a knight.

4

You can dress up as a princess.

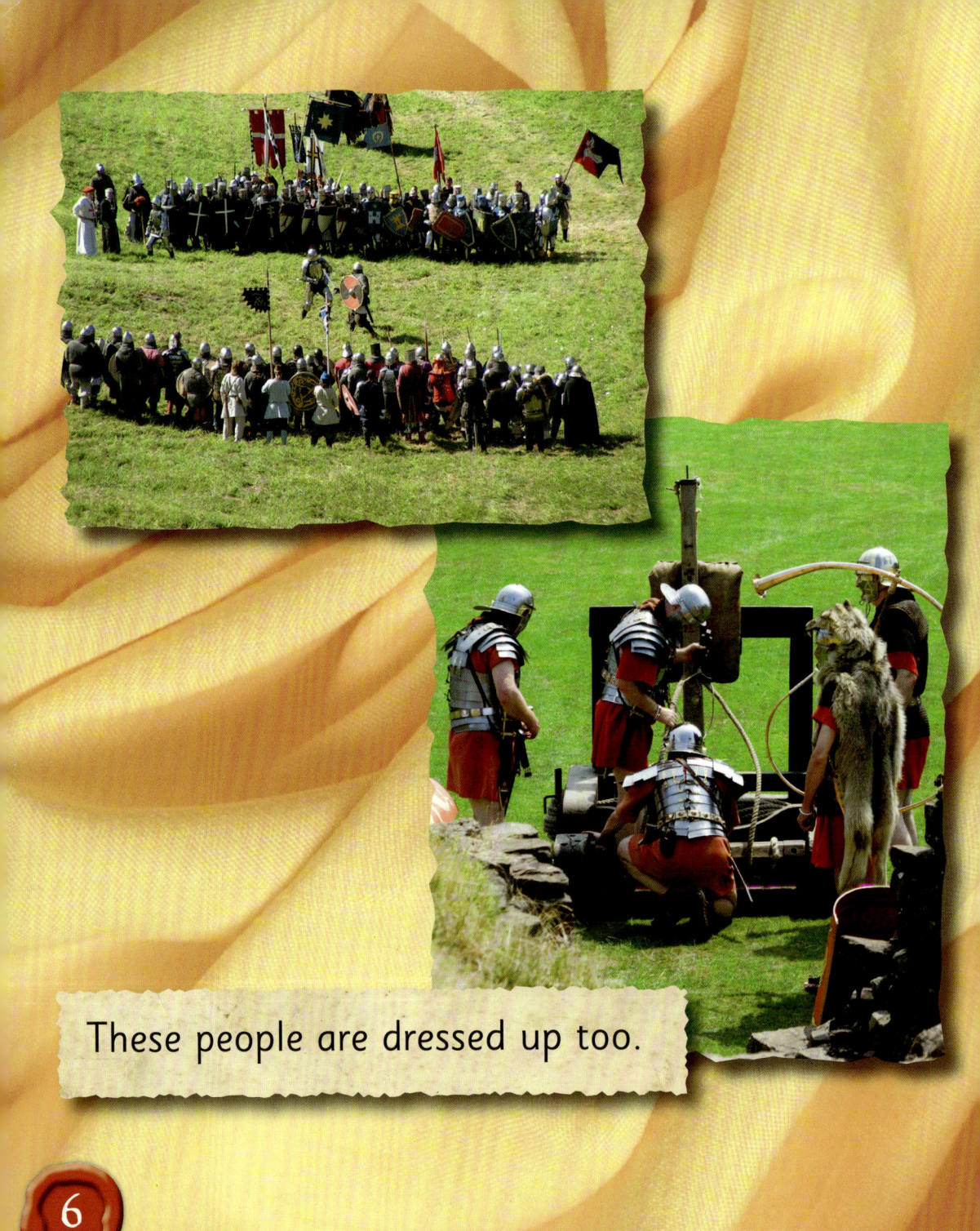

These people are dressed up too.

But long ago, people used to wear clothes like these every day!

Queen

The big collar she is wearing is called a ruff.

This queen is wearing these clothes for a special occasion.

These clothes also keep her warm when it is cold in the castle.

This queen has a lot of jewellery. She keeps it locked in her jewellery box.

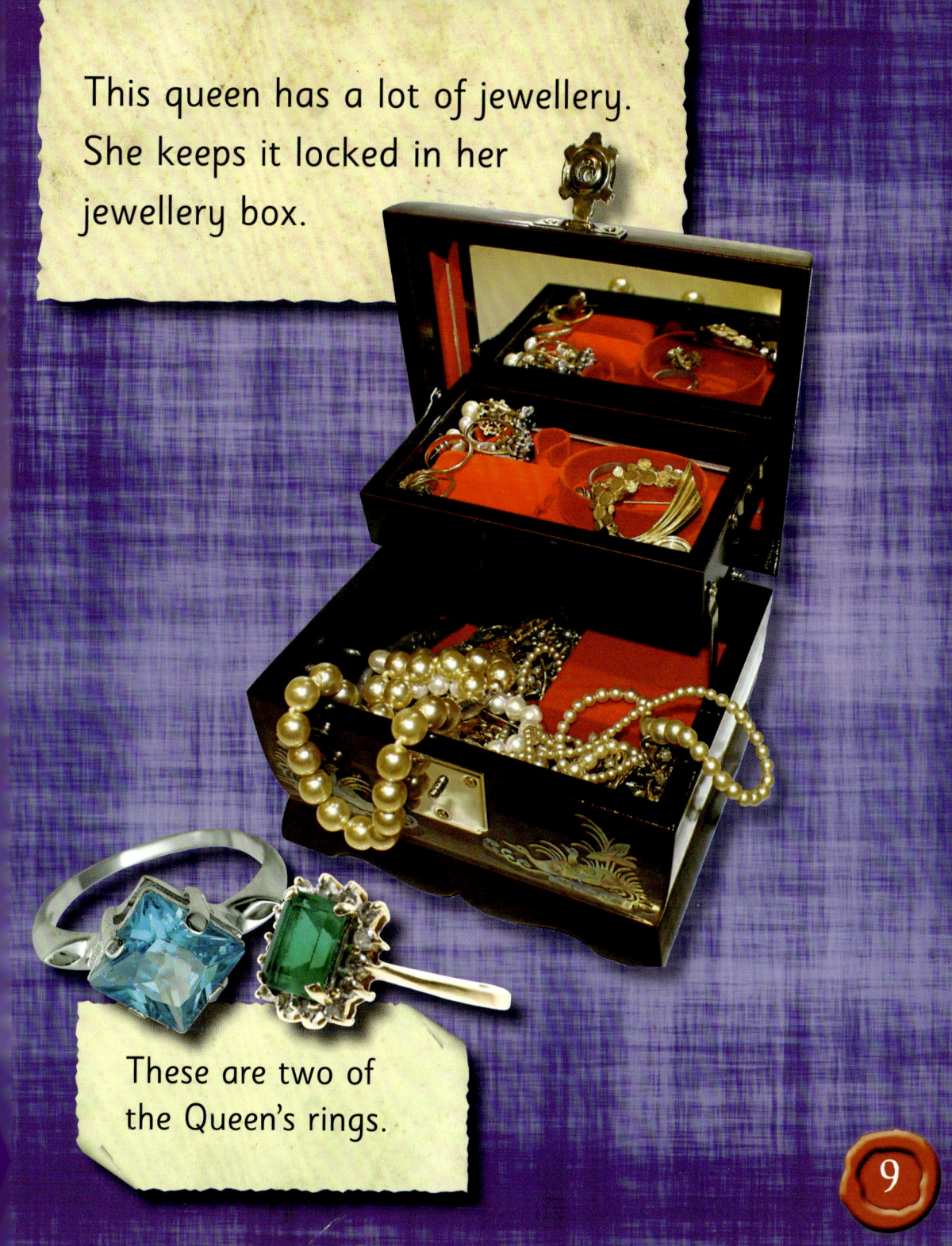

These are two of the Queen's rings.

King

This king is dressed in his robes.

They are made of special cloth.

He is carrying a sceptre (say sep-ter).

The sceptre shows how important he is.

The king has a crown to show how important he is.

This crown is made of gold and jewels.

Princess

This princess is going to a special dance, called a ball.

She is wearing her best ball gown.

Sometimes this princess wears a tiara.
A tiara is a kind of crown.

This tiara is made of silver and jewels.

Prince

This prince is wearing a special head dress. It is called a turban.

His clothes show how important he is.

Some princes wear a crown instead of a turban.

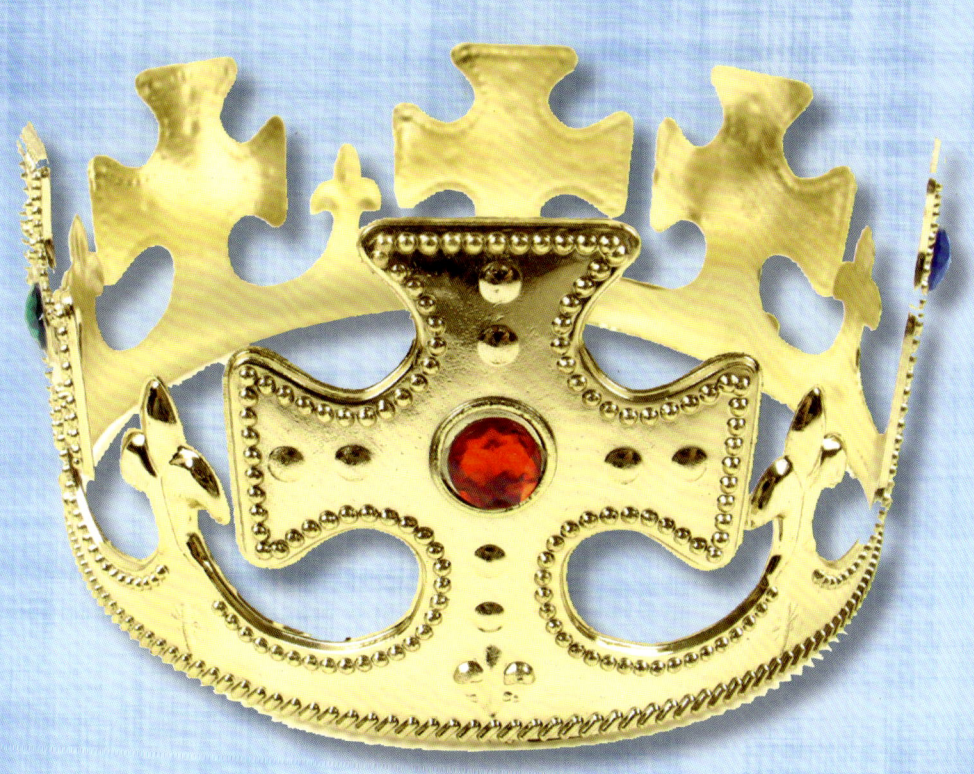

Knights

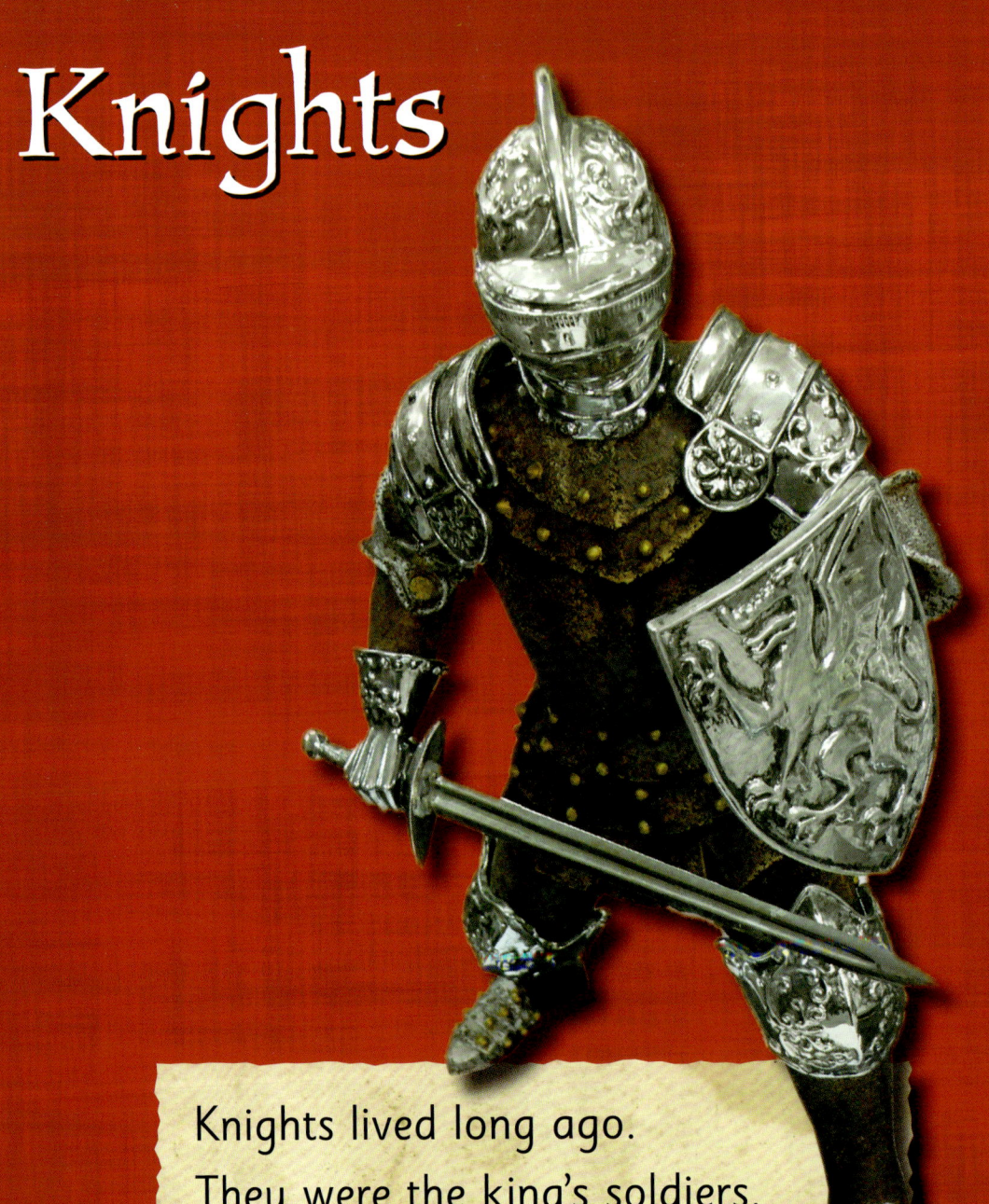

Knights lived long ago.
They were the king's soldiers.

They wore special metal clothes to protect them.

They also used shields to protect themselves.

A knight's metal clothes are called a suit of armour.

It was very hot and heavy to wear.

A suit of armour

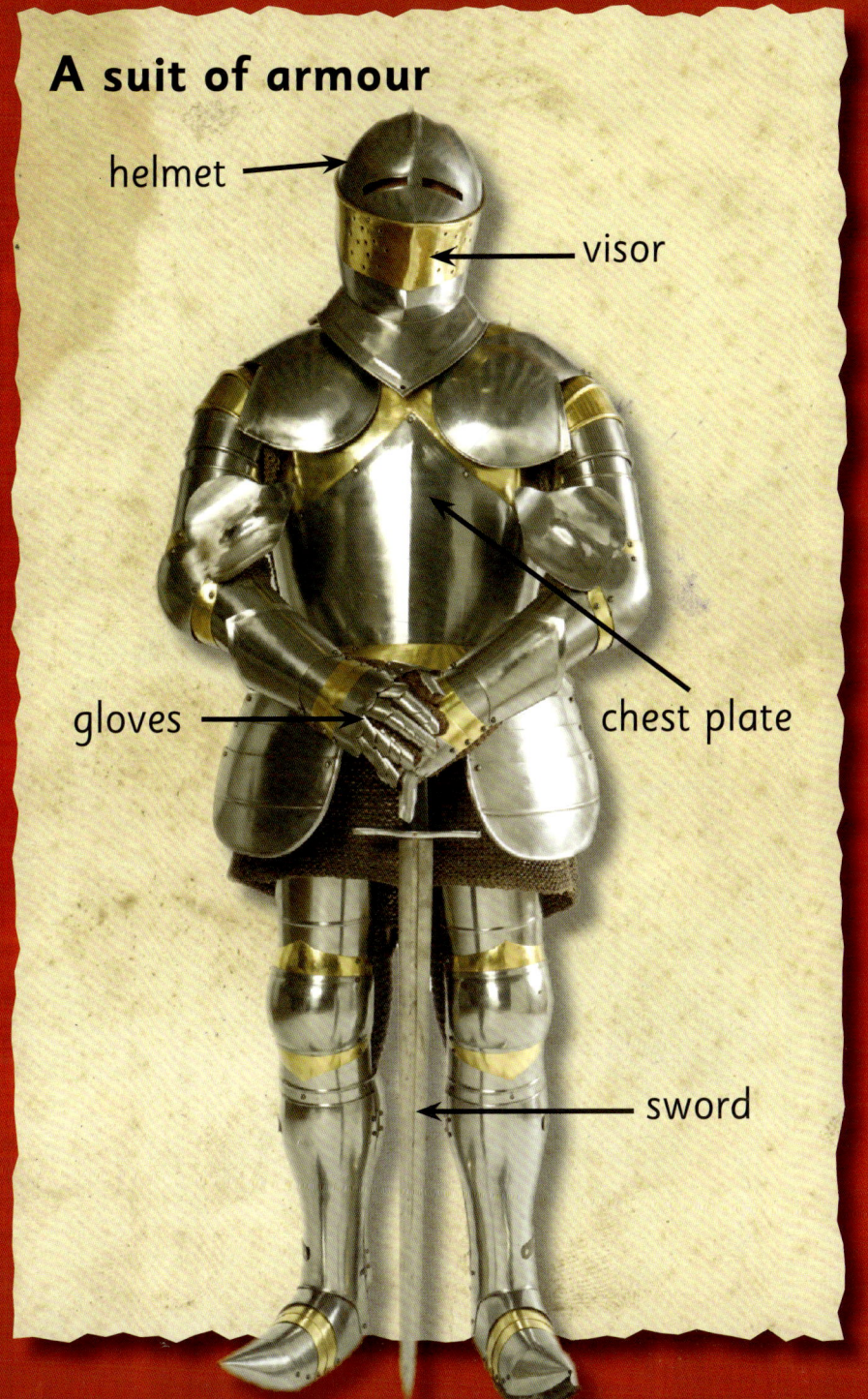

- helmet
- visor
- gloves
- chest plate
- sword

A knight wore a special long top over his armour.

It was called a tabard.

Each knight had a different picture or pattern on his tabard.

The pattern on the tabard was also on the knight's shield and his horse.

Quiz

1 Who wears this turban?

2 Who wears this helmet?

③ Who wears this tiara?

④ Who wears this ruff?

⑤ Who carries this sceptre?

Answers

1. A prince is wearing this turban.

2. This helmet belongs to a knight.

3. This tiara belongs to a princess.

4. A queen is wearing this ruff.

5. The king is carrying a sceptre.